# My WAGON TRAIN ADVENTURE

By Lynda Arnéz

**Please visit our website, www.garethstevens.com. For a free color catalog of all our high-quality books, call toll free 1-800-542-2595 or fax 1-877-542-2596.**

Library of Congress Cataloging-in-Publication Data

Names: Arnéz, Lynda.
Title: My wagon train adventure / Lynda Arnéz.
Description: New York : Gareth Stevens Pub., 2016. | Series: My place in
  history | Includes index.
Identifiers: LCCN 2015034678 | ISBN 9781482440027 (pbk.) | ISBN 9781482440034 (6 pack) | ISBN 9781482440041
(library bound)
Subjects: LCSH: Pioneer children–West (U.S.)–Juvenile literature. |
  Overland journeys to the Pacific–Juvenile literature. | Pioneers–West
  (U.S.)–Juvenile literature. | Frontier and pioneer life–West
  (U.S.)–Juvenile literature. | West (U.S.)–Social life and customs–19th
  century–Juvenile literature.
Classification: LCC F596 .A7175 2016 | DDC 978/.02–dc23
LC record available at http://lccn.loc.gov/2015034678

First Edition

Published in 2016 by
**Gareth Stevens Publishing**
111 East 14th Street, Suite 349
New York, NY 10003

Copyright © 2016 Gareth Stevens Publishing

Designer: Laura Bowen
Editor: Kristen Nelson

Photo credits: Cover, pp. 1 (pioneer family), 7 (inset) Underwood Archives/Archive Photos/Getty Images; cover,
pp. 1–24 (torn strip) barbaliss/Shutterstock.com; cover, pp. 1–24 (photo frame) Davor Ratkovic/Shutterstock.com; cover,
pp. 1–24 (white paper) HABRDA/Shutterstock.com; cover, pp. 1–24 (parchment) M. Unal Ozmen/Shutterstock.com; cover,
pp. 1–24 (textured edge) saki80/Shutterstock.com; cover (background) Natalia Sheinkin/Shutterstock.com; pp. 1–24
(paper background) Kostenko Maxim/Shutterstock.com; p. 7 (main) Transcendental Graphics/Archive Photos/Getty
Images; p. 9 Kean Collection/Archive Photos/Getty Images; p. 11 De Agostini Picture Library/De Agostini/Getty Images;
p. 13 (main) J. Norman Reid/Shutterstock.com; p. 13 (inset) sergioboccardo/Shutterstock.com; pp. 15, 17 (main), 19, 21
MPI/Stringer/Archive Photos/Getty Images; p. 17 (inset) FTH/Shutterstock.com.

Printed in the United States of America

CPSIA compliance information: Batch #CW16GS: For further information contact Gareth Stevens, New York, New York at 1-800-542-2595.

# CONTENTS

Words in the glossary appear in **bold** type the first time they are used in the text.

# JUMPING OFF

April 20, 1843

Today marks the beginning of our trip west! Mother told me that since I'm the best at writing, I'm who should keep the family journal. I'll do the best I can!

We've left behind my grandparents and most of my cousins in St. Louis, Missouri. My older brother is very upset because he had to leave his friends. My best friend, Violet, and her family have come to Independence, Missouri, with us and will be going all the way to Oregon Country, too. I'm lucky!

## Notes from History

In 1843, about 1,000 pioneers headed west on the Oregon Trail from Independence. The trail was one of the main pathways for wagon trains going west until the 1860s.

# THE OREGON TRAIL

Oregon City, Oregon

Independence, Missouri

Many pioneers had to first travel to "jumping off" points like Independence to meet up with others going west. For some, this was a hard journey.

# Leaving
# MORE BEHIND

April 30, 1843

   The start to our journey has been hard. After a few days, our group realized the wagons were too heavy for the oxen to pull for so many miles! Mother had to put Grandmother's dish set on the side of the trail. I had to leave all my books except the Bible. Mother said I'll start my schooling again when we get to Oregon.

   We walk next to the wagon. Father says we're only allowed to ride in it if we're sick or hurt.

## Notes from History

In order to survive the journey of 4 or 5 months to California or Oregon, pioneers had to pack hundreds of pounds of flour and bacon, as well as sugar, coffee, **lard**, beans, and rice.

The most common type of covered wagon used to travel the Oregon Trail was called a Prairie Schooner. It could hold up to 2,500 pounds (1,134 kg) of supplies.

May 13, 1843

I might have more **chores** on the trail than at home!

Most mornings I get up very early and start making breakfast

with Mother. I'm already tired of eating bacon! Violet and I

have to milk our families' cows every morning.

After helping our mothers wash and put away

the dishes, we get water, firewood,

and bison chips. That's

bison poop! It burns

well and helps keep

us warm at night, so I

don't mind picking it up.

## Notes from History

Children traveling by wagon train played with each other and their families' animals. There was plenty of time for fun, such as singing and dancing around the campfire.

In general, men drove the wagons, guarded the camp at night, and hunted for extra food. Women sometimes helped with this in addition to caring for children, washing clothes, and cooking.

# ACCIDENT!

June 2, 1843

A girl I know was injured today. She was walking next to her family's wagon when her skirt got caught in the wheel. The wagon ran over her leg and broke it!

This wasn't the first time someone has gotten hurt by the wagon wheels, but she's the first person I know who's been in a serious **accident**. Father said a little boy was killed soon after we left Independence. He fell out of the wagon! I'm going to be much more careful.

## Notes from History

Guns going off accidentally was another way pioneers might be hurt on the wagon train.

Thousands of pioneers were buried along the Oregon Trail after dying from an accident or an illness such as dysentery or mountain fever.

# Bison SIGHTING

June 18, 1843

    We've been on the trail for about 2 months, and we finally spotted a herd of bison! I've seen a few at a time, but there were hundreds of them. My mother thought there might be rain coming because we heard thunder. She was wrong! The thunder was the sound of the herd coming toward us!

    Father and a few of the men shot and killed a bison for us to eat. Mother thinks it's wasteful because we can't **preserve** the leftover meat.

## Notes from History

Pioneers hunted and fished along the Oregon Trail whenever they could to make their supplies last the whole trip.

When most **emigrants** were
using the Oregon Trail between
1843 and the 1860s, there were
millions of bison on the US plains.
In the following years, these animals
were killed in large numbers.

# A Friendly TRADE

July 2, 1843

Yesterday was both scary and exciting. We met our first Indians! Back in St. Louis, many people told Father to be careful crossing Indian land on the Oregon Trail. They said we would be attacked!

The Indians we met were friendly. They wanted to trade with us! Father got Mother and me soft shoes called moccasins. They're made out of animal **hide**. My shoes have been worn out from all the walking, so the moccasins are so comfortable! The Indians didn't stay long, but I'm much less afraid now.

### Notes from History

The pioneers were crossing through land that had belonged to Native Americans for thousands of years. Some native peoples were upset by this and did attack wagon trains.

Pioneers who reached the Columbia River were able
to trade with Native Americans there for salmon.

# Bread AND BUTTER

July 19, 1843

Today was a great day! I've gotten very tired of eating the same thing all the time—bacon, dried fruit, beans, and fried "Johnny cakes" made with flour and water. But today, Mother made bread!

It's hard to bake anything at camp. When we stop for the night, there's not usually enough time. Mother made the bread dough right away so it would have time to rise. She baked it in a **Dutch oven** borrowed from another family.

## Notes from History

Pioneers had fresh butter with their bread! They put the cream from cows' milk in a covered bucket under the wagon where it was knocked around enough to **churn** it into butter.

When the emigrants set up camp each night, they tried to be near water for washing and drinking.

DUTCH OVEN

# The HARDEST PART

August 14, 1843

    I've never seen mountains as big as these! Father said the hardest part of our journey is crossing these mountains. We left one of our two oxen behind at the foot of the mountains. He was too worn out to make it.

    Violet's family lost their whole wagon a few days ago. The trail was so steep, Violet's father lost control at the top. He broke his arm jumping out. We helped them gather what they could from the crash.

## Notes from History

Losing an ox, cow, or sheep was common. The trip on a wagon train was as hard for animals as it was for people.

Traveling the Oregon Trail was hard—but the worst part of it wasn't until near the end, when pioneers had to cross the Cascade Mountains to reach their new home.

September 3, 1843

Oregon City isn't very far now. My older brother says he can't wait to meet new people. Father and Mother are excited for more land and the opportunity for what they call a "better life."

I'm just happy we made it the whole way together. I turned 9 years old last week when we were just getting out of the mountains. I couldn't believe how different this birthday was from last year's! What will my birthday be like next year?

## Notes from History

Oregon wasn't the only **destination** for pioneers on the Oregon Trail. They also settled in present-day Washington State, California, Nevada, Idaho, and Utah.

# The Oregon Trail by the Numbers

- The Oregon Trail was almost **2,000 miles** (3,220 km) from Missouri to Willamette Valley in Oregon.

- The first people to travel to Oregon in a covered wagon made the trip in **1836**.

- Wagon trains commonly traveled **10 to 15 miles** (16 to 24 km) each day.

- About **40,000** emigrants were children.

- At least **20,000** people died and were buried along the Oregon Trail.

# GLOSSARY

**accident:** an unexpected event that happens by chance

**chore:** a task

**churn:** to stir or shake forcefully

**destination:** the place to which somebody or something is going

**Dutch oven:** a covered pot made of iron that is used for baking on an open fire

**emigrant:** someone who leaves his or her native land to live in another country

**hide:** the skin of an animal

**lard:** fat from some animals used for cooking

**pioneer:** one of the first American settlers to travel to and settle in the West

**preserve:** to stop from going bad

# For more INFORMATION

## Books

Aronin, Miriam. *How Many People Traveled the Oregon Trail? And Other Questions About the Trail West.* Minneapolis, MN: Lerner Publications, 2012.

Hester, Sallie. *Diary of Sallie Hester: A Covered Wagon Girl.* North Mankato, MN: Capstone Press, 2014.

Kravitz, Danny. *Surviving the Journey: The Story of the Oregon Trail.* North Mankato, MN: Capstone Press, 2015.

## Websites

**Pathways of Pioneers**
*video.idahoptv.org/video/2167662782/*
Watch a video about the pioneers journeying across Idaho and the hardships they faced.

**Westward Expansion: Oregon Trail**
*www.ducksters.com/history/westward_expansion/oregon_trail.php*
Read more about traveling the Oregon Trail and the westward expansion of the United States.

# INDEX